Justin Martyr:
The Discourse to the Greeks
And Hortatory Address to
the Greeks

Justin Martyr: The Discourse to the Greeks and Hortatory Address to the Greeks

Justin Martyr

Justin Martyr: The Discourse to the Greeks and Hortatory Address to the Greeks

© Lighthouse Publishing 2020

Written by: Justin Martyr 100 – 165 AD
Translated by: Rev. M. Dods, M.A. 1834 - 1909
Updated into Modern U.S English: A.M. Overett (b. 1960)

All rights reserved. Without limiting the rights under copyright reserved above, no part of this publication may be reproduced, stored in a retrieval system, or transmitted, in any form or by any means (electronic, mechanical, photocopying, recording or otherwise), without the prior written permission of the copyright owner of this book.

Published by
Lighthouse Publishing
SAN 257-4330
5531 Dufferin Drive
Savage, Minnesota, 55378
United States of America

www.lighthouseebooks.com

The Discourse to the Greeks

Chapter I.—Justin justifies his departure from Greek customs.

Do not suppose, ye Greeks, that my separation from your customs is unreasonable and unthinking; for I found in them nothing that is holy or acceptable to God. For the very compositions of your poets are monuments of madness and intemperance. For anyone who becomes the scholar of your most eminent instructor, is more beset by difficulties than all men besides. For first they say that Agamemnon, abetting the extravagant lust of his brother, and his madness and unrestrained desire, readily gave even his daughter to be sacrificed, and troubled all Greece that he might rescue Helen, who had been ravished by the leprous shepherd. But when in the course of the war they took captives, Agamemnon was himself taken captive by Chryseis, and for Briseis' sake kindled a feud with the son of Thetis. And Pelides himself, who crossed the river, overthrew Troy, and subdued Hector, this your hero became the slave of Polyxena, and was conquered by a dead Amazon; and putting off the god-fabricated armor, and donning the hymeneal robe, he became a sacrifice of love in the temple of Apollo. And the Ithacan Ulysses made a virtue of a vice. And indeed his sailing past the Sirens gave evidence that he was destitute of worthy prudence, because he could not depend on his prudence for stopping his ears. Ajax, son of Telamon, who bore the shield of sevenfold ox-hide, went mad when he was defeated in the contest with Ulysses for the armor. Such things I have no desire to be instructed in. Of such virtue I am not covetous, that I should believe the myths of Homer. For the whole rhapsody, the beginning and end both of the Iliad and the Odyssey is—a woman.

Chapter II.—The Greek Theogony exposed.

But since, next to Homer, Hesiod wrote his Works and Days, who will believe his driveling theogony? For they say that Chronos, the son of Ouranos, in the beginning slew his father, and possessed himself of his rule; and that, being seized with a panic lest he should himself suffer in the same way, he preferred devouring his children; but that, by the craft of the Curetes, Jupiter was conveyed away and kept in secret, and afterwards bound his father with chains, and divided the empire; Jupiter receiving, as the story goes, the air, and Neptune the deep, and Pluto the portion of Hades. But Pluto ravished Proserpine; and Ceres sought her child wandering through the deserts. And this myth was celebrated in the Eleusinian fire. Again, Neptune ravished Melanippe when she was drawing water, besides abusing a host of Nereids not a few, whose names, were we to recount them, would cost us a multitude of words. And as for Jupiter, he was a various adulterer, with Antiope as a satyr, with Danaë as gold, and with Europa as a bull; with Leda, moreover, he assumed wings. For the love of Semele proved both his unchastity and the jealousy of Semele. And they say that he carried off the Phrygian Ganymede to be his cup-bearer. These, then, are the exploits of the sons of Saturn. And your illustrious son of Latona [Apollo], who professed soothsaying, convicted himself of lying. He pursued Daphne, but did not gain possession of her; and to Hyacinthus, who loved him, he did not foretell his death. And I say nothing of the masculine character of

Minerva, nor of the feminine nature of Bacchus, nor of the fornicating disposition of Venus. Read to Jupiter, ye Greeks, the law against parricides, and the penalty of adultery, and the ignominy of pæderasty. Teach Minerva and Diana the works of women, and Bacchus the works of men. What seemliness is there in a woman's girding herself with armor, or in a man's decorating himself with cymbals, and garlands, and female attire, and accompanied by a herd of bacchanalian women?

Chapter III.—Follies of the Greek mythology.

For Hercules, celebrated by his three nights, sung by the poets for his successful labors, the son of Jupiter, who slew the lion and destroyed the many-headed hydra; who put to death the fierce and mighty boar, and was able to kill the fleet man-eating birds, and brought up from Hades the three-headed dog; who effectually cleansed the huge Augean building from its dung, and killed the bulls and the stag whose nostrils breathed fire, and plucked the golden fruit from the tree, and slew the poisonous serpent (and for some reason, which it is not lawful to utter, killed Achelous, and the guest-slaying Busiris), and crossed the mountains that he might get water which gave forth an articulate speech, as the story goes: he who was able to do so many and such like and so great deeds as these, how childishly he was delighted to be stunned by the cymbals of the satyrs, and to be conquered by the love of woman, and to be struck on the hips by the laughing Lyda! And at last, not being able to put off the tunic of Nessus, himself kindling his own funeral pile, so he died. Let Vulcan lay aside his envy, and not be jealous if he is hated because he is old and club-footed, and Mars loved, because young and beautiful. Since, therefore, ye Greeks, your gods are convicted of intemperance, and your heroes are effeminate, as the histories on which your dramas are founded have declared, such as the curse of Atreus, the bed of Thyestes and the taint in the house of Pelops, and Danaus murdering through hatred and making Ægyptus childless in the intoxication of his rage, and the Thyestean banquet spread by the Furies. And Procne is to this day flitting about, lamenting; and her sister of Athens shrills with her tongue cut out. For what need is there of speaking of the goad of Œdipus, and the murder of Laius, and the marrying his mother, and the mutual slaughter of those who were at once his brothers and his sons?

Chapter IV.—Shameless practices of the Greeks.

And your public assemblies I have come to hate. For there are excessive banqueting, and subtle flutes which provoke to lustful movements, and useless and luxurious anointing, and crowning with garlands. With such a mass of evils do you banish shame; and ye fill your minds with them, and are carried away by intemperance, and indulge as a common practice in wicked and insane fornication. And this further I would say to you, why are you, being a Greek, indignant at your son when he imitates Jupiter, and rises against you and defrauds you of your own wife? Why do you count him your enemy, and yet worship one that is like him? And why do you blame your wife for living in unchastity, and yet honor Venus with shrines? If indeed these things had been related by others, they would have seemed to be mere slanderous accusations, and not truth. But now your own poets sing these things, and your histories noisily publish them.

Chapter V.—Closing appeal.

Henceforth, ye Greeks, come and partake of incomparable wisdom, and be instructed by the Divine Word, and acquaint yourselves with the King immortal; and do not recognize those men as heroes who slaughter whole nations. For our own Ruler, the Divine Word, who even now constantly aids us, does not desire strength of body and beauty of feature, nor yet the high spirit of earth's nobility, but a pure soul, fortified by holiness, and the watchwords of our King, holy actions, for through the Word power passes into the soul. O trumpet of peace to the soul that is at war! O weapon that putts to flight terrible passions! O instruction that quenches the innate fire of the soul! The Word exercises an influence which does not make poets: it does not equip philosophers nor skilled orators, but by its instruction it makes mortals immortal, mortals gods; and from the earth transports them to the realms above Olympus. Come, be taught; become as I am, for I, too, was as ye are. These have conquered me—the divinity of the instruction, and the power of the Word: for as a skilled serpent-charmer lures the terrible reptile from his den and causes it to flee, so the Word drives the fearful passions of our sensual nature from the very recesses of the soul; first driving forth lust, through which every ill is begotten—hatreds, strife, envy, emulations, anger, and such like. Lust being once banished, the soul becomes calm and serene. And being set free from the ills in which it was sunk up to the neck, it returns to Him who made it. For it is fit that it be restored to that state whence it departed, whence every soul was or is.

Justin's Hortatory Address to the Greeks

Chapter I.—Reasons for addressing the Greeks.

As I begin this hortatory address to you, ye men of Greece, I pray God that I may know what I ought to say to you, and that you, shaking off your habitual love of disputing, and being delivered from the error of your fathers, may now choose what is profitable; not fancying that you commit any offence against your forefathers, though the things which you formerly considered by no means salutary should now seem useful to you. For accurate investigation of matters, putting truth to the question with a more searching scrutiny, often reveals that things which have passed for excellent are of quite another sort. Since, then, we propose to discourse of the true religion (than which, I think, there is nothing which is counted more valuable by those who desire to pass through life without danger, on account of the judgment which is to be after the termination of this life, and which is announced not only by our forefathers according to God, to wit the prophets and lawgivers, but also by those among yourselves who have been esteemed wise, not poets alone, but also philosophers, who professed among you that they had attained the true and divine knowledge), I think it well first of all to examine the teachers of religion, both our own and yours, who they were, and how great, and in what times they lived; in order that those who have formerly received from their fathers the false religion, may now, when they perceive this, be extricated from that inveterate error; and that we may clearly and manifestly show that we ourselves follow the religion of our forefathers according to God.

Chapter II—The poets are unfit to be religious teachers.

Whom, then, ye men of Greece, do ye call your teachers of religion? The poets? It will do your cause no good to say so to men who know the poets; for they know how very ridiculous a theogony they have composed,—as we can learn from Homer, your most distinguished and prince of poets. For he says, first, that the gods were in the beginning generated from water; for he has written thus:—

"Both ocean, the origin of the gods, and their mother Tethys"

And then we must also remind you of what he further says of him whom ye consider the first of the gods, and whom he often calls "the father of gods and men;" for he said: —

"Zeus, who is the dispenser of war to men."

Indeed, he says that he was not only the dispenser of war to the army, but also the cause of perjury to the Trojans, by means of his daughter; and Homer introduces him in love, and bitterly complaining, and bewailing himself, and plotted against by the other gods, and at one time exclaiming concerning his own son:—

"Alas! He falls, my most beloved of men!
Sarpedon, vanquished by Patroclus, falls.
So will the fates."

And at another time concerning Hector: —

"Ah! I behold a warrior dear to me
Around the walls of Ilium driven, and grieve
For Hector."

And what he says of the conspiracy of the other gods against Zeus, they know who read these words: "When the other Olympians—Juno, and Neptune, and Minerva —wished to bind him." And unless the blessed gods had feared him whom gods call Briareus, Zeus would have been bound by them. And what Homer says of his intemperate loves, we must remind you in the very words he used. For he said that Zeus spoke thus to Juno:—

"For never goddess pour'd, nor woman yet,
So full a tide of love into my breast;
I never loved Ixion's consort thus,
Nor sweet Acrisian Danaë, from whom
Sprang Perseus, noblest of the race of man;
Nor Phœnix' daughter fair, of whom were born
Minos, unmatch'd but by the powers above,
And Rhadamanthus; nor yet Semele,
Nor yet Alcmene, who in Thebes produced
The valiant Hercules; and though my son
By Semele were Bacchus, joy of man;

Nor Ceres golden-hair'd, nor high-enthron'd
Latona in the skies; no—nor thyself
As now I love thee, and my soul perceive
O'erwhelm'd with sweetness of intense desire."

It is fit that we now mention what one can learn from the work of Homer of the other gods, and what they suffered at the hands of men. For he says that Mars and Venus were wounded by Diomed, and of many others of the gods he relates the sufferings. For thus we can gather from the case of Dione consoling her daughter; for she said to her:—

"Have patience, dearest child; though much enforc'd
Restrain thine anger: we, in heav'n who dwell,
Have much to bear from mortals; and ourselves
Too oft upon each other suff'rings lay:
Mars had his suff'rings; by Alöeus sons,
Otus and Ephialtes, strongly bound,
He thirteen months in brazen fetters lay:
Juno, too, suffer'd, when Amphitryon's son
Thro' her right breast a three-barb'd arrow sent:
Dire, and unheard of, were the pangs she bore,
Great Pluto's self the stinging arrow felt,
When that same son of Ægis-bearing Jove
Assail'd him in the very gates of hell,
And wrought him keenest anguish; pierced with pain,
To high Olympus, to the courts of Jove,
Groaning, he came; the bitter shaft remain'd
Deep in his shoulder fix'd, and griev'd his soul."

But if it is right to remind you of the battle of the gods, opposed to one another, your own poet himself will recount it, saying:—

"Such was the shock when gods in battle met;
For there to royal Neptune stood oppos'd
Phœbus Apollo with his arrows keen;
The blue-eyed Pallas to the god of war;
To Juno, Dian, heav'nly archeress,
Sister of Phœbus, golden-shafted queen.
Stout Hermes, helpful god, Latona fac'd."

These and such like things did Homer teach you; and not Homer only, but also Hesiod. So that if you believe your most distinguished poets, who have given the genealogies of your gods, you must of necessity either suppose that the gods are such beings as these, or believe that there are no gods at all.

Chapter III.—Opinions of the school of Thales.

And if you decline citing the poets, because you say it is allowable for them to frame myths, and to relate in a mythical way many things about the gods which are far from true, do you suppose you have some others for your religious teachers, or how do you say that they themselves have learned this religion of yours? For it is impossible that any should know matters so great and divine, who have not themselves learned them first from the initiated. You will no doubt say, "The sages and philosophers." For to them, as to a fortified wall, you are wont to flee, when any one quotes the opinions of your poets about the gods. Therefore, since it is fit that we commence with the ancients and the earliest, beginning thence I will produce the opinion of each, much more ridiculous as it is than the theology of the poets. For Thales of Miletus, who took the lead in the study of natural philosophy, declared that water was the first principle of all things; for from water he says that all things are, and that into water all are resolved. And after him Anaximander, who came from the same Miletus, said that the infinite was the first principle of all things; for that from this indeed all things are produced, and into this do all decay. Thirdly, Anaximenes—and he too was from Miletus—says that air is the first principle of all things; for he says that from this all things are produced, and into this all are resolved. Heraclitus and Hippasus, from Metapontus, say that fire is the first principle of all things; for from fire all things proceed, and in fire do all things terminate. Anaxagoras of Clazomenæ said that the homogeneous parts are the first principles of all things. Archelaus, the son of Apollodorus, an Athenian, says that the infinite air and its density and rarity are the first principle of all things. All these, forming a succession from Thales, followed the philosophy called by themselves physical.

Chapter IV.—Opinions of Pythagoras and Epicurus.

Then, in regular succession from another starting-point, Pythagoras the Samian, son of Mnesarchus, calls numbers, with their proportions and harmonies, and the elements composed of both, the first principles; and he includes also unity and the indefinite binary. Epicurus, an Athenian, the son of Neocles, says that the first principles of the things that exist are bodies perceptible by reason, admitting no vacuity, unbegotten, indestructible, which can neither be broken, nor admit of any formation of their parts, nor alteration, and are therefore perceptible by reason. Empedocles of Agrigentum, son of Meton, maintained that there were four elements—fire, air, water, earth; and two elementary powers —love and hate, of which the former is a power of union, the latter of separation. You see, then, the confusion of those who are considered by you to have been wise men, whom you assert to be your teachers of religion: some of them declaring that water is the first principle of all things; others, air others, fire; and others, some other of these fore-mentioned elements; and all of them employing persuasive arguments for the establishment of their own errors, and attempting to prove their own peculiar dogma to be the most valuable. These things were said by them. How then, ye men of Greece, can it be safe for those who desire to be saved, to fancy that they can learn the true religion from these philosophers, who were neither able so to convince themselves as to prevent sectarian wrangling with one another, and not to appear definitely opposed to one another's opinions?

Chapter V.—Opinions of Plato and Aristotle.

But possibly those who are unwilling to give up the ancient and inveterate error, maintain that they have received the doctrine of their religion not from those who have now been mentioned, but from those who are esteemed among them as the most renowned and finished philosophers, Plato and Aristotle. For these, they say, have learned the perfect and true religion. But I would be glad to ask, first of all, from those who say so, from whom they say that these men have learned this knowledge; for it is impossible that men who have not learned these so great and divine matters from some who knew them, should either themselves know them, or be able correctly to teach others; and, in the second place, I think we ought to examine the opinions even of these sages. For we shall see whether each of these does not manifestly contradict the other. But if we find that even they do not agree with each other, I think it is easy to see clearly that they too are ignorant. For Plato, with the air of one that has descended from above, and has accurately ascertained and seen all that is in heaven, says that the most high God exists in a fiery substance. But Aristotle, in a book addressed to Alexander of Macedon, giving a compendious explanation of his own philosophy, clearly and manifestly overthrows the opinion of Plato, saying that God does not exist in a fiery substance: but inventing, as a fifth substance, some kind ofætherial and unchangeable body, says that God exists in it. Thus, at least, he wrote: "Not, as some of those who have erred regarding the Deity say, that God exists in a fiery substance." Then, as if he were not satisfied with this blasphemy against Plato, he further, for the sake of proving what he says about the ætherial body, cites as a witness him whom Plato had banished from his republic as a liar, and as being an imitator of the images of truth at three removes, for so Plato calls Homer; for he wrote: "Thus at least did Homer speak, 'And Zeus obtained the wide heaven in the air and the clouds,' " wishing to make his own opinion appear more worthy of credit by the testimony of Homer; not being aware that if he used Homer as a witness to prove that he spoke truth, many of his tenets would be proved untrue. For Thales of Miletus, who was the founder of philosophy among them, taking occasion from him, will contradict his first opinions about first principles. For Aristotle himself, having said that God and matter are the first principles of all things, Thales, the eldest of all their sages, says that water is the first principle of the things that exist; for he says that all things are from water, and that all things are resolved into water. And he conjectures this, first, from the fact that the seed of all living creatures, which is their first principle, is moist; and secondly, because all plants grow and bear fruit in moisture, but when deprived of moisture, wither. Then, as if not satisfied with his conjectures, he cites Homer as a most trustworthy testimony, who speaks thus:—

"Ocean, who is the origin of all."

May not Thales, then, very fairly say to him, "What is the reason, Aristotle, why you give heed to Homer, as if he spoke truth, when you wish to demolish the opinions of Plato; but when you promulgate an opinion contrary to ours, you think Homer untruthful?"

Chapter VI.—Further disagreements between Plato and Aristotle.

And that these very wonderful sages of yours do not even agree in other respects, can be easily learned from this. For while Plato says that there are three first principles of all things, God, and matter, and form,—God, the maker of all; and matter, which is the subject of the first production of all that is produced, and affords to God opportunity for His workmanship; and form, which is the type of each of the things produced, — Aristotle makes no mention at all of form as a first principle, but says that there are two, God and matter. And again, while Plato says that the highest God and the ideas exist in the first place of the highest heavens, and in fixed sphere, Aristotle says that, next to the most high God, there are, not ideas, but certain gods, who can be perceived by the mind. Thus, then, do they differ concerning things heavenly. So that one can see that they not only are unable to understand our earthly matters, but also, being at variance among themselves regarding these things, they will appear unworthy of credit when they treat of things heavenly. And that even their doctrine regarding the human soul as it now is does not harmonize, is manifest from what has been said by each of them concerning it. For Plato says that it is of three parts, having the faculty of reason, of affection, and of appetite. But Aristotle says that the soul is not so comprehensive as to include also corruptible parts, but only reason. And Plato loudly maintains that "the whole soul is immortal." But Aristotle, naming it "the actuality," would have it to be mortal, not immortal. And the former says it is always in motion; but Aristotle says that it is immoveable, since it must itself precede all motion.

Chapter VII.—Inconsistencies of Plato's doctrine.

But in these things they are convicted of thinking in contradiction to each other. And if anyone will accurately criticize their writings, they have chosen to abide in harmony not even with their own opinions. Plato, at any rate, at one time says that there are three first principles of the universe—God, and matter, and form; but at another time four, for he adds the universal soul. And again, when he has already said that matter is eternal, he afterwards says that it is produced; and when he has first given to form its peculiar rank as a first principle, and has asserted for its self-subsistence, he afterwards says that this same thing is among the things perceived by the understanding. Moreover, having first declared that everything that is made is mortal he afterwards states that some of the things that are made are indestructible and immortal. What, then, is the cause why those who have been esteemed wise among you disagree not only with one another but also with themselves? Manifestly, their unwillingness to learn from those who know, and their desire to attain accurate knowledge of things heavenly by their own human excess of wisdom though they were able to understand not even earthly matters. Certainly some of your philosophers say that the human soul is in us; others, that it is around us. For not even in this did they choose to agree with one another, but, distributing, as it were, ignorance in various ways among themselves, they thought fit to wrangle and dispute with one another even about the soul. For some of them say that the soul is fire, and some that it is the air; and others, the mind; and others, motion; and others, an exhalation; and certain others say that it is a power flowing from the stars; and others, number capable of motion; and others, a generating water. And a wholly confused and inharmonious opinion has prevailed among them, which only in this one respect appears praiseworthy to those who can form a right judgment, that they have been anxious to convict one another of error and falsehood.

Chapter VIII.—Antiquity, inspiration, and harmony of Christian teachers.

Since therefore it is impossible to learn anything true concerning religion from your teachers, who by their mutual disagreement have furnished you with sufficient proof of their own ignorance, I consider it reasonable to recur to our progenitors, who both in point of time have by a great way the precedence of your teachers, and who have taught us nothing from their own private fancy, nor differed with one another, nor attempted to overturn one another's positions, but without wrangling and contention received from God the knowledge which also they taught to us. For neither by nature nor by human conception is it possible for men to know things so great and divine, but by the gift which then descended from above upon the holy men, who had no need of rhetorical art, nor of uttering anything in a contentious or quarrelsome manner, but to present themselves pure to the energy of the Divine Spirit, in order that the divine plectrum itself, descending from heaven, and using righteous men as an instrument like a harp or lyre, might reveal to us the knowledge of things divine and heavenly. Wherefore, as if with one mouth and one tongue, they have in succession, and in harmony with one another, taught us both concerning God, and the creation of the world, and the formation of man, and concerning the immortality of the human soul, and the judgment which is to be after this life, and concerning all things which it is needful for us to know, and thus in divers times and places have afforded us the divine instruction.

Chapter IX.—The antiquity of Moses proved by Greek writers.

I will begin, then, with our first prophet and lawgiver, Moses; first explaining the times in which he lived, on authorities which among you are worthy of all credit. For I do not propose to prove these things only from our own divine histories, which as yet you are unwilling to credit on account of the inveterate error of your forefathers, but also from your own histories, and such, too, as have no reference to our worship, that you may know that, of all your teachers, whether sages, poets, historians, philosophers, or lawgivers, by far the oldest, as the Greek histories show us, was Moses, who was our first religious teacher. For in the times of Ogyges and Inachus, whom some of your poets supposed to have been earth-born, Moses is mentioned as the leader and ruler of the Jewish nation. For in this way he is mentioned both by Polemon in the first book of his Hellenics, and by Apion son of Posidonius in his book against the Jews, and in the fourth book of his history, where he says that during the reign of Inachus over Argos the Jews revolted from Amasis king of the Egyptians, and that Moses led them. And Ptolemæus the Mendesian, in relating the history of Egypt, concurs in all this. And those who write the Athenian history, Hellanicus and Philochorus (the author of The Attic History), Castor and Thallus and Alexander Polyhistor, and also the very well informed writers on Jewish affairs, Philo and Josephus, have mentioned Moses as a very ancient and time-honored prince of the

Jews. Josephus, certainly, desiring to signify even by the title of his work the antiquity and age of the history, wrote thus at the commencement of the history: "The Jewish antiquities of Flavius Josephus,"—signifying the oldness of the history by the word "antiquities." And your most renowned historian Diodorus, who employed thirty whole years in epitomizing the libraries, and who, as he himself wrote, travelled over both Asia and Europe for the sake of great accuracy, and thus became an eye-witness of very many things, wrote forty entire books of his own history. And he in the first book, having said that he had learned from the Egyptian priests that Moses was an ancient lawgiver, and even the first, wrote of him in these very words: "For subsequent to the ancient manner of living in Egypt which gods and heroes are fabled to have regulated, they say that Moses first persuaded the people to use written laws, and to live by them; and he is recorded to have been a man both great of soul and of great faculty in social matters." Then, having proceeded a little further, and wishing to mention the ancient lawgivers, he mentions Moses first. For he spoke in these words: "Among the Jews they say that Moses ascribed his laws to that God who is called Jehovah, whether because they judged it a marvelous and quite divine conception which promised to benefit a multitude of men, or because they were of opinion that the people would be the more obedient when they contemplated the majesty and power of those who were said to have invented the laws. And they say that Sasunchis was the second Egyptian legislator, a man of excellent understanding. And the third, they say, was Sesonchosis the king, who not only performed the most brilliant military exploits of any in Egypt, but also consolidated that warlike race by legislation. And the fourth lawgiver, they say, was Bocchoris the king, a wise and surpassingly skillful man. And after him it is said that Amasis the king acceded to the government, whom they relate to have regulated all that pertains to the rulers of provinces, and to the general administration of the government of Egypt. And they say that Darius, the father of Xerxes, was the sixth who legislated for the Egyptians."

Chapter X—Training and inspiration of Moses.

These things, ye men of Greece, have been recorded in writing concerning the antiquity of Moses by those who were not of our religion; and they said that they learned all these things from the Egyptian priests, among whom Moses was not only born, but also was thought worthy of partaking of all the education of the Egyptians, on account of his being adopted by the king's daughter as her son; and for the same reason was thought worthy of great attention, as the wisest of the historians relate, who have chosen to record his life and actions, and the rank of his descent, —I speak of Philo and Josephus. For these, in their narration of the history of the Jews, say that Moses was sprung from the race of the Chaldæans, and that he was born in Egypt when his forefathers had migrated on account of famine from Phœnicia to that country; and him God chose to honor on account of his exceeding virtue, and judged him worthy to become the leader and lawgiver of his own race, when He thought it right that the people of the Hebrews should return out of Egypt into their own land. To him first did God communicate that divine and prophetic gift which in those days descended upon the holy men, and him also did He first furnish that he might be our teacher in religion, and then after him the rest of the prophets, who both obtained the same gift as he, and taught us the same doctrines concerning the same subjects. These we assert to have been our teachers, who taught us nothing from their own human conception, but from the gift vouchsafed to them by God from above.

Chapter XI.—Heathen oracles testify of Moses.

But as you do not see the necessity of giving up the ancient error of your forefathers in obedience to these teachers [of ours], what teachers of your own do you maintain to have lived worthy of credit in the matter of religion? For, as I have frequently said, it is impossible that those who have not themselves learned these so great and divine things from such persons as are acquainted with them, should either themselves know them, or be able rightly to teach others. Since, therefore, it has been sufficiently proved that the opinions of your philosophers are obviously full of all ignorance and deceit, having now perhaps wholly abandoned the philosophers as formerly you abandoned the poets, you will turn to the deceit of the oracles; for in this style I have heard some speaking. Therefore I think it fit to tell you at this step in our discourse what I formerly heard among you concerning their utterances. For when one inquired at your oracle—it is your own story—what religious men had at any time happened to live, you say that the oracle answered thus: "Only the Chaldæans have obtained wisdom, and the Hebrews, who worship God Himself, the self-begotten King."

Since, therefore, you think that the truth can be learned from your oracles, when you read the histories and what has been written regarding the life of Moses by those who do not belong to our religion, and when you know that Moses and the rest of the prophets were descended from the race of the Chaldæans and Hebrews, do not think that anything incredible has taken place if a man sprung from a godly line, and who lived worthily of the godliness of his fathers, was chosen by God to be honored with this great gift and to be set forth as the first of all the prophets.

Chapter XII.—Antiquity of Moses proved.

And I think it necessary also to consider the times in which your philosophers lived, that you may see that the time which produced them for you is very recent, and also short. For thus you will be able easily to recognize also the antiquity of Moses. But lest, by a complete survey of the periods, and by the use of a greater number of proofs, I should seem to be prolix, I think it may be sufficiently demonstrated from the following. For Socrates was the teacher of Plato, and Plato of Aristotle. Now these men flourished in the time of Philip and Alexander of Macedon, in which time also the Athenian orators flourished, as the Philippics of Demosthenes plainly show us. And those who have narrated the deeds of Alexander sufficiently prove that during his reign Aristotle associated with him. From all manner of proofs, then, it is easy to see that the history of Moses is by far more ancient than all profane histories. And, besides, it is fit that you recognize this fact also, that nothing has been accurately recorded by Greeks before the era of the Olympiads, and that there is no ancient work which makes known any action of the Greeks or Barbarians. But before that period existed only the history of the prophet Moses, which he wrote in the Hebrew character by the divine inspiration. For the Greek character was not yet in use, as the teachers of language themselves prove, telling us that Cadmus first brought the letters from Phœnicia, and communicated them to the Greeks. And your first of philosophers, Plato, testifies that they were a recent discovery. For in the Timæus he wrote that Solon, the wisest of the wise men, on his return from Egypt, said to Critias that he had heard this from a very aged Egyptian priest, who said to him, "O Solon, Solon, you Greeks are ever children, and aged Greek there is none." Then again he said, "You are all youths in soul, for you hold no ancient opinion derived through remote tradition, nor any system of instruction hoary with time; but all these things escape your knowledge, because for many generations the posterity of these ancient ages died mute, not having the use of letters." It is fit, therefore, that you understand that it is the fact that every history has been written in these recently-discovered Greek letters; and if anyone would make mention of old poets, or legislators, or historians, or philosophers, or orators, he will find that they wrote their own works in the Greek character.

Chapter XIII.—History of the Septuagint.

But if anyone says that the writings of Moses and of the rest of the prophets were also written in the Greek character, let him read profane histories, and know that Ptolemy, king of Egypt, when he had built the library in Alexandria, and by gathering books from every quarter had filled it, then learnt that very ancient histories written in Hebrew happened to be carefully preserved; and wishing to know their contents, he sent for seventy wise men from Jerusalem, who were acquainted with both the Greek and Hebrew language, and appointed them to translate the books; and that in freedom from all disturbance they might the more speedily complete the translation, he ordered that there should be constructed, not in the city itself, but seven stadia off (where the Pharos was built), as many little cots as there were translators, so that each by himself might complete his own translation; and enjoined upon those officers who were appointed to this duty, to afford them all attendance, but to prevent communication with one another, in order that the accuracy of the translation might be discernible even by their agreement. And when he ascertained that the seventy men had not only given the same meaning, but had employed the same words, and had failed in agreement with one another not even to the extent of one word; but had written the same things, and concerning the same things, he was struck with amazement, and believed that the translation had been written by divine power, and perceived that the men were worthy of all honor, as beloved of God, and with many gifts ordered them to return to their own country. And having, as was natural, marveled at the books, and concluded them to be divine, he consecrated them in that library. These things, ye men of Greece, are no fable, nor do we narrate fictions; but we ourselves having been in Alexandria, saw the remains of the little cots at the Pharos still preserved, and having heard these things from the inhabitants, who had received them as part of their country's tradition, we now tell to you what you can also learn from others, and specially from those wise and esteemed men who have written of these things, Philo and Josephus, and many others. But if any of those who are wont to be forward in contradiction should say that these books do not belong to us, but to the Jews, and should assert that we in vain profess to have learnt our religion froth them, let him know, as he may from those very things which are written in these books, that not to them, but to us, does the doctrine of them refer. That the books relating to our religion are to this day preserved among the Jews, has been a work of Divine Providence on our behalf; for lest, by producing them out of the Church, we should give occasion to those who wish to slander us to charge us with fraud, we demand that they be produced from the synagogue of the Jews, that from the very books still preserved among them it might clearly and evidently appear, that the laws which were written by holy men for instruction pertain to us.

Chapter XIV.—A warning appeal to the Greeks.

It is therefore necessary, ye Greeks, that you contemplate the things that are to be, and consider the judgment which is predicted by all, not only by the godly, but also by those who are irreligious, that ye do not without investigation commit yourselves to the error of your fathers, nor suppose that if they themselves have been in error, and have transmitted it to you, that this which they have taught you is true; but looking to the danger of so terrible a mistake, inquire and investigate carefully into those things which are, as you say, spoken of even by your own teachers. For even unwillingly they were on your account forced to say many things by the Divine regard for mankind, especially those of them who were in Egypt, and profited by the godliness of Moses and his ancestry. For I think that some of you, when you read even carelessly the history of Diodorus, and of those others who wrote of these things, cannot fail to see that both Orpheus, and Homer, and Solon, who wrote the laws of the Athenians, and Pythagoras, and Plato, and some others, when they had been in Egypt, and had taken advantage of the history of Moses, afterwards published doctrines concerning the gods quite contrary to those which formerly they had erroneously promulgated.

Chapter XV.—Testimony of Orpheus to monotheism.

At all events, we must remind you what Orpheus, who was, as one might say, your first teacher of polytheism, latterly addressed to his son Musæus, and to the other legitimate auditors, concerning the one and only God. And he spoke thus:—
"I speak to those who lawfully may hear:
All others, ye profane, now close the doors,
And, O Musæus! hearken thou to me,
Who offspring art of the light-bringing moon:
The words I utter now are true indeed;
And if thou former thoughts of mine hast seen,
Let them not rob thee of the blessed life,
But rather turn the depths of thine own heart
Unto the place where light and knowledge dwell.
Take thou the word divine to guide thy steps,
And walking well in the straight certain path,
Look to the one and universal King—
One, self-begotten, and the only One,
Of whom all things and we ourselves are sprung.
All things are open to His piercing gaze,
While He Himself is still invisible.

Present in all His works, though still unseen,
He gives to mortals evil out of good,
Sending both chilling wars and tearful griefs;
And other than the great King there is none.
The clouds forever settle round His throne,
And mortal eyeballs in mere mortal eyes
Are weak, to see Jove reigning over all.
He sits established in the brazen heavens
Upon His golden throne; under His feet
He treads the earth, and stretches His right hand
To all the ends of ocean, and around
Tremble the mountain ranges and the streams,
The depths, too, of the blue and hoary sea."

And again, in some other place he says:—

"There is one Zeus alone, one sun, one hell,
One Bacchus; and in all things but one God;

Nor of all these as diverse let me speak."

And when he swears he says:—

"Now I adjure thee by the highest heaven,
The work of the great God, the only wise;
And I adjure thee by the Father's voice.
Which first He uttered when He stablished
The whole world by His counsel."

What does he mean by "I adjure thee by the Father's voice, which first He uttered?" It is the Word of God which he here names "the voice," by whom heaven and earth and the whole creation were made, as the divine prophecies of the holy men teach us; and these he himself also paid some attention to in Egypt, and understood that all creation was made by the Word of God; and therefore, after he says, "I adjure thee by the Father's voice, which first He uttered," he adds this besides, "when by His counsel He established the whole world." Here he calls the Word "voice," for the sake of the poetical meter. And that this is so, is manifest from the fact, that a little further on, where the meter permits him, he names it "Word." For he said:—

"Take thou the Word divine to guide thy steps."

Chapter XVI.—Testimony of the Sibyl.

We must also mention what the ancient and exceedingly remote Sibyl, whom Plato and Aristophanes, and others besides, mention as a prophetess, taught you in her oracular verses concerning one only God. And she speaks thus:—

"There is one only unbegotten God,
Omnipotent, invisible, most high,
All-seeing, but Himself seen by no flesh."

Then elsewhere thus:—

"But we have strayed from the Immortal's ways,
And worship with a dull and senseless mind
Idols, the workmanship of our own hands,
And images and figures of dead men."

And again somewhere else:—

"Blessed shall be those men upon the earth
Who shall love the great God before all else,
Blessing Him when they eat and when they drink;
Trusting it, this their piety alone.
Who shall abjure all shrines which they may see,
All altars and vain figures of dumb stones,
Worthless and stained with blood of animals,
And sacrifice of the four-fooled tribes,
Beholding the great glory of One God."

These are the Sibyl's words.

Chapter XVII.—Testimony of Homer.

And the poet Homer, using the license of poetry, and rivalling the original opinion of Orpheus regarding the plurality of the gods, mentions, indeed, several gods in a mythical style, lest he should seem to sing in a different strain from the poem of Orpheus, which he so distinctly proposed to rival, that even in the first line of his poem he indicated the relation he held to him. For as Orpheus in the beginning of his poem had said, "O goddess, sing the wrath of Demeter, who brings the goodly fruit," Homer began thus, "O goddess, sing the wrath of Achilles, son of Peleus," preferring, as it seems to me, even to violate the poetical meter in his first line, than that he should seem not to have remembered before all else the names of the gods. But shortly after he also clearly and explicitly presents his own opinion regarding one God only, somewhere saying to Achilles by the mouth of Phœnix, "Not though God Himself were to promise that He would peel off my old age, and give me the rigor of my youth," where he indicates by the pronoun the real and true God. And somewhere he makes Ulysses address the host of the Greeks thus: "The rule of many is not a good thing; let there be one ruler." And that the rule of many is not a good thing, but on the contrary an evil, he proposed to evince by fact, recounting the wars which took place on account of the multitude of rulers, and the fights and factions, and their mutual counterplots. For monarchy is free from contention. So far the poet Homer.

Chapter XVIII.—Testimony of Sophocles.

And if it is needful that we add testimonies concerning one God, even from the dramatists, hear even Sophocles speaking thus:—

"There is one God, in truth there is but one,
Who made the heavens and the broad earth beneath,
The glancing waves of ocean and the winds
But many of us mortals err in heart,
And set up for a solace in our woes
Images of the gods in stone and wood,
Or figures carved in brass or ivory,
And, furnishing for these our handiworks,
Both sacrifice and rite magnificent,
We think that thus we do a pious work."

Thus, then, Sophocles.

Chapter XIX.—Testimony of Pythagoras.

And Pythagoras, son of Mnesarchus, who

expounded the doctrines of his own philosophy, mystically by means of symbols, as those who have written his life show, himself seems to have entertained thoughts about the unity of God not unworthy of his foreign residence in Egypt. For when he says that unity is the first principle of all things, and that it is the cause of all good, he teaches by an allegory that God is one, and alone. And that this is so, is evident from his saying that unity and one differ widely from one another. For he says that unity belongs to the class of things perceived by the mind, but that one belongs to numbers. And if you desire to see a clearer proof of the opinion of Pythagoras concerning one God, hear his own opinion, for he spoke as follows: "God is one; and He Himself does not, as some suppose, exist outside the world, but in it, He being wholly present in the whole circle, and beholding all generations; being the regulating ingredient of all the ages, and the administrator of His own powers and works, the first principle of all things, the light of heaven, and Father of all, the intelligence and animating soul of the universe, the movement of all orbits." Thus, then, Pythagoras.

Chapter XX.—Testimony of Plato.

But Plato, though he accepted, as is likely, the doctrine of Moses and the other prophets regarding one only God, which he learned while in Egypt, yet fearing, on account of what had befallen Socrates, lest he also should raise up some Anytus or Meletus against himself, who should accuse him before the Athenians, and say, "Plato is doing harm, and making himself mischievously busy, not acknowledging the gods recognized by the state;" in fear of the hemlock-juice, contrives an elaborate and ambiguous discourse concerning the gods, furnishing by his treatise gods to those who wish them, and none for those who are differently disposed, as may readily be seen from his own statements. For when he has laid down that everything that is made is mortal, he afterwards says that the gods were made. If, then, he would have God and matter to be the origin of all things, manifestly it is inevitably necessary to say that the gods were made of matter; but if of matter, out of which he said that evil also had its origin, he leaves right-thinking persons to consider what kind of beings the gods should be thought who are produced out of matter. For, for this very reason did he say that matter was eternal, that he might not seem to say that God is the creator of evil. And regarding the gods who were made by God, there is no doubt he said this: "Gods of gods, of whom I am the creator." And he manifestly held the correct opinion concerning the really existing God. For having heard in Egypt that God had said to Moses, when He was about to send him to the Hebrews, "I am that I am," he understood that God had not mentioned to him His own proper name.

Chapter XXI.—The namelessness of God.

For God cannot be called by any proper name, for names are given to mark out and distinguish their subject-matters, because these are many and diverse; but neither did anyone exist before God who could give Him a name, nor did He Himself think it right to name Himself, seeing that He is one and unique, as He Himself also by His own prophets testifies, when He says, "I God am the first," and after this, "And beside me there is no other God." On this account, then, as I before said, God did not, when He sent Moses to the Hebrews, mention any name, but by a participle He mystically teaches them that He is the one and only God. "For," says He; "I am the Being;" manifestly contrasting Himself, "the Being," with those who are not, that those who had hitherto been deceived might see that they were attaching themselves, not to beings, but to those who had no being. Since, therefore, God knew that the first men remembered the old delusion of their forefathers, whereby the misanthropic demon contrived to deceive them when he said to them, "If ye obey me in transgressing the commandment of God, ye shall be as gods," calling those gods which had no being, in order that men, supposing that there were other gods in existence, might believe that they themselves could become gods. On this account He said to Moses, "I am the Being," that by the participle "being" He might teach the difference between God who is and those who are not.786 Men, therefore, having been duped by the deceiving demon, and having dared to disobey God, were cast out of Paradise, remembering the name of gods, but no longer being taught by God that there are no other gods. For it was not just that they who did not keep the first commandment, which it was easy to keep, should any longer be taught, but should rather be driven to just punishment. Being therefore banished from Paradise, and thinking that they were expelled on account of their disobedience only, not knowing that it was also because they had believed in the existence of gods which did not exist, they gave the name of gods even to the men who were afterwards born of themselves. This first false fancy, therefore, concerning gods, had its origin with the father of lies. God, therefore, knowing that the false opinion about the plurality of gods was burdening the soul of man like some disease, and wishing to remove and eradicate it, appeared first to Moses, and said to him, "I am He who is." For it was necessary, I think, that he who was to be the ruler and leader of the Hebrew people should first of all know the living God. Wherefore, having appeared to him first, as it was possible for God to appear to a man, He said to him, "I am He who is;" then, being about to send him to the Hebrews, He further orders him to say, "He who is hath sent me to you."

Chapter XXII.—Studied ambiguity of Plato.

Plato accordingly having learned this in Egypt, and being greatly taken with what was said about one God, did indeed consider it unsafe to mention the name of Moses, on account of his teaching the doctrine of one only God, for he dreaded the Areopagus; but what is very well expressed by him in his elaborate treatise, the Timæus, he has written in exact correspondence with what Moses said regarding God, though he has done so, not as if he had learned it from him, but as if he were expressing his own opinion. For he said, "In my opinion, then, we must first define what that is which exists eternally, and has no generation, and what that is which is always being generated, but never really is." Does not this, ye men of Greece, seem to those who are able to understand the matter to be one and the same thing, saving only the difference of the article? For Moses said, "He who is," and Plato, "That which is." But either of the expressions seems to apply to the ever-existent God. For He is the only one who eternally exists, and has no generation. What, then, that other thing is which is contrasted with the ever-existent, and of which he said, "And what that is which is always being generated, but never really is," we must attentively consider. For we shall find him clearly and evidently saying that He who is unbegotten is eternal, but that those that are begotten and made are generated and perish—as he said of the same class, "gods of gods, of whom I am maker"—for he speaks in the following words: "In my opinion, then, we must first define what that is which is always existent and has no birth, and what that is which is always being generated but never really is. The former, indeed, which is apprehended by reflection combined with reason, always exists in the same way; while the latter, on the other hand, is conjectured by opinion formed by the perception of the senses unaided by reason, since it never really is, but is coming into being and perishing." These expressions declare to those who can rightly understand them the death and destruction of the gods that have been brought into being. And I think it necessary to attend to this also, that Plato never names him the creator, but the fashioner of the gods, although, in the opinion of Plato, there is considerable difference between these two. For the creator creates the creature by his own capability and power, being in need of nothing else; but the fashioner frames his production when he has received from matter the capability for his work.

Chapter XXIII.—Plato's self-contradiction.

But, perhaps, some who are unwilling to abandon the doctrines of polytheism, will say that to these fashioned gods the maker said, "Since ye have been produced, ye are not immortal, nor at all, imperishable;

yet shall ye not perish nor succumb to the fatality of death, because you have obtained my will, which is a still greater and mightier bond." Here Plato, through fear of the adherents of polytheism, introduces his "maker" uttering words which contradict himself. For having formerly stated that he said that everything which is produced is perishable, he now introduces him saying the very opposite; and he does not see that it is thus absolutely impossible for him to escape the charge of falsehood. For he either at first uttered what is false when he said that everything which is produced is perishable, or now, when he propounds the very opposite to what he had formerly said. For if, according to his former definition, it is absolutely necessary that every created thing be perishable, how can he consistently make that possible which is absolutely impossible? So that Plato seems to grant an empty and impossible prerogative to his "maker," when he propounds that those who were once perishable because made from matter should again, by his intervention, become imperishable and enduring. For it is quite natural that the power of matter, which, according to Plato's opinion, is uncreated, and contemporary and coæval with the maker, should resist his will. For he who has not created has no power, in respect of that which is uncreated, so that it is not possible that it (matter), being free, can be controlled by any external necessity. Wherefore Plato himself, in consideration of this, has written thus: "It is necessary to affirm that God cannot suffer violence."

Chapter XXIV.—Agreement of Plato and Homer.

How, then, does Plato banish Homer from his

republic, since, in the embassy to Achilles, he represents Phœnix as saying to Achilles, "Even the gods themselves are not inflexible," though Homer said this not of the king and Platonic maker of the gods, but of some of the multitude whom the Greeks esteem as gods, as one can gather from Plato's saying, "gods of gods?" For Homer, by that golden chain, refers all power and might to the one highest God. And the rest of the gods, he said, were so far distant from his divinity that he thought fit to name them even along with men. At least he introduces Ulysses saying of Hector to Achilles, "He is raging terribly, trusting in Zeus, and values neither men nor gods." In this passage Homer seems to me without doubt to have learnt in Egypt, like Plato, concerning the one God, and plainly and openly to declare this, that he who trusts in the really existent God makes no account of those that do not exist. For thus the poet, in another passage, and employing another but equivalent word, to wit, a pronoun, made use of the same participle employed by Plato to designate the really existent God, concerning whom Plato said, "What that is which always exists, and has no birth." For not without a double sense does this expression of Phœnix seem to have been used: "Not even if God Himself were to promise me, that, having burnished off my old age, He should set me forth in the flower of youth." For the pronoun "Himself" signifies the really existing God. For thus, too, the oracle which was given to you concerning the Chaldæans and Hebrews signifies. For when someone inquired what men had ever lived godly, you say the answer was:—

"Only the Chaldæans and the Hebrews found wisdom,

Worshipping God Himself, the unbegotten King."

Chapter XXV.—Plato's knowledge of God's eternity.

How, then, does Plato blame Homer for saying that the gods are not inflexible, although, as is obvious from the expressions used, Homer said this for a useful purpose? For it is the property of those who expect to obtain mercy by prayer and sacrifices, to cease from and repent of their sins. For those who think that the Deity is inflexible, are by no means moved to abandon their sins, since they suppose that they will derive no benefit from repentance. How, then, does Plato the philosopher condemn the poet Homer for saying, "Even the gods themselves are not inflexible," and yet himself represent the maker of the gods as so easily turned, that he sometimes declares the gods to be mortal, and at other times declares the same to be immortal? And not only concerning them, but also concerning matter, from which, as he says, it is necessary that the created gods have been produced, he sometimes says that it is uncreated, and at other times that it is created; and yet he does not see that he himself, when he says that the maker of the gods is so easily turned, is convicted of having fallen into the very errors for which he blames Homer, though Homer said the very opposite concerning the maker of the gods. For he said that he spoke thus of himself:—

"For ne'er my promise shall deceive, or fail,
Or be recall'd, if with a nod confirm'd."

But Plato, as it seems, unwillingly entered not these strange dissertations concerning the gods, for he feared those who were attached to polytheism. And whatever he thinks fit to tell of all that he had learned from Moses and the prophets concerning one God, he preferred delivering in a mystical style, so that those who desired to be worshippers of God might have an inkling of his own opinion. For being charmed with that saying of God to Moses, "I am the really existing," and accepting with a great deal of thought the brief participial expression, he understood that God desired to signify to Moses His eternity, and therefore said, "I am the really existing;" for this word "existing" expresses not one time only, but the three—the past, the present, and the future. For when Plato says, "And which never really is," he uses the verb "is" of time indefinite. For the word "never" is not spoken, as some suppose, of the past, but of the future time. And this has been accurately understood even by profane writers. And therefore, when Plato wished, as it were, to interpret to the uninitiated what had been mystically expressed by the participle concerning the eternity of God, he employed the following language: "God indeed, as the old tradition runs, includes the beginning, and end, and middle of all things." In this sentence he plainly and obviously names the law of Moses "the old tradition," fearing, through dread of the hemlock-cup, to mention the name of Moses; for he understood that the teaching of the man was hateful to the Greeks; and he clearly enough indicates Moses by the antiquity of the tradition. And we have sufficiently proved from Diodorus and the rest of the historians, in the foregoing chapters, that the law of Moses is not only old, but even the first. For Diodorus says that he was the first of all lawgivers; the letters which belong to the Greeks, and which they employed in the writing of their histories, having not yet been discovered.

Chapter XXVI.—Plato indebted to the prophets.

And let no one wonder that Plato should believe Moses regarding the eternity of God. For you will find him mystically referring the true knowledge of realities to the prophets, next in order after the really existent God. For, discoursing in the Timæus about certain first principles, he wrote thus: "This we lay down as the first principle of fire and the other bodies, proceeding according to probability and necessity. But the first principles of these again God above knows, and whosoever among men is beloved of Him." And what men does he think beloved of God, but Moses and the rest of the prophets? For their prophecies he read, and, having learned from them the doctrine of the judgment, he thus proclaims it in the first book of the Republic: "When a man begins to think he is soon to die, fear invades him, and concern about things which had never before entered his head. And those stories about what goes on in Hades, which tell us that the man who has here been unjust must there be punished, though formerly ridiculed, now torment his soul with apprehensions that they may be true. And he, either through the feebleness of age, or even because he is now nearer to the things of the other world, views them more attentively. He becomes, therefore, full of apprehension and dread, and begins to call himself to account and to consider whether he has done any one an injury. And that man who finds in his life many iniquities, and who continually starts from his sleep as children do, lives in terror, and with a forlorn prospect. But to him who is conscious of no wrong-doing, sweet hope is the constant companion and good nurse of old age, as Pindar says. For this, Socrates, he has elegantly expressed, that 'whoever leads a life of holiness and justice, him sweet hope, the nurse of age, accompanies, cheering his heart, for she powerfully sways the changeful mind of mortals.' " This Plato wrote in the first book of the Republic.

Chapter XXVII.—Plato's knowledge of the judgment.

And in the tenth book he plainly and manifestly wrote what he had learned from the prophets about the judgment, not as if he had learned it from them, but, on account of his fear of the Greeks, as if he had heard it from a man who has been slain in battle—for this story he thought fit to invent—and who, when he was about to be buried on the twelfth day, and was lying on the funeral pile, came to life again, and described the other world. The following are his very words: "For he said that he was present when one was asked by another person where the great Ardiæus was. This Ardiæus had been prince in a certain city of Pamphylia, and had killed his aged father and his elder brother, and done many other unhallowed deeds, as was reported. He said, then that the person who was asked said: He neither comes nor ever will come hither. For we saw, among other terrible sights, this also. When we were close to the mouth [of the pit], and were about to return to the upper air, and had suffered everything else, we suddenly beheld both him and others likewise, most of whom were tyrants. But there were also some private sinners who had committed great crimes.

And these, when they thought they were to ascend, the mouth would not permit, but bellowed when any of those who were so incurably wicked attempted to ascend, unless they had paid the full penalty. Then fierce men, fiery to look at, stood close by, and hearing the din, took some and led them away; but Ardiæus and the rest, having bound hand and foot, and striking their heads down, and flaying, they dragged to the road outside, tearing them with thorns, and signifying to those who were present the cause of their suffering these things, and that they were leading them away to cast them into Tartarus. Hence, he said, that amidst all their various fears, this one was the greatest, lest the mouth should bellow when they ascended, since if it were silent each one would most gladly ascend; and that the punishments and torments were such as these, and that, on the other hand, the rewards were the reverse of these." Here Plato seems to me to have learnt from the prophets not only the doctrine of the judgment, but also of the resurrection, which the Greeks refuse to believe. For his saying that the soul is judged along with the body, proves nothing more clearly than that he believed the doctrine of the resurrection. Since how could Ardiæus and the rest have undergone such punishment in Hades, had they left on earth the body, with its head, hands, feet, and skin? For certainly they will never say that the soul has a head and hands, and feet and skin. But Plato, having fallen in with the testimonies of the prophets in Egypt, and having accepted what they teach concerning the resurrection of the body, teaches that the soul is judged in company with the body.

Chapter XXVIII.—Homer's obligations to the sacred writers.

And not only Plato, but Homer also, having received similar enlightenment in Egypt, said that Tityus was in like manner punished. For Ulysses speaks thus to Alcinous when he is recounting his divination by the shades of the dead:—

"There Tityus, large and long, in fetters bound,
O'erspread nine acres of infernal ground;
Two ravenous vultures, furious for their food,
Scream o'er the fiend, and riot in his blood,
Incessant gore the liver in his breast,
Th' immortal liver grows, and gives th' immortal feast."

For it is plain that it is not the soul, but the body, which has a liver. And in the same manner he has described both Sisyphus and Tantalus as enduring punishment with the body. And that Homer had been in Egypt, and introduced into his own poem much of what he there learnt, Diodorus, the most esteemed of historians, plainly enough teaches us. For he said that when he was in Egypt he had learnt that Helen, having received from Theon's wife, Polydamna, a drug, "lulling all sorrow and melancholy, and causing forgetfulness of all ills," brought it to Sparta. And Homer said that by making use of that drug Helen put an end to the lamentation of Menelaus, caused by the presence of Telemachus. And he also called

Venus "golden," from what he had seen in Egypt. For he had seen the temple which in Egypt is called "the temple of golden Venus," and the plain which is named "the plain of golden Venus." And why do I now make mention of this? To show that the poet transferred to his own poem much of what is contained in the divine writings of the prophets. And first he transferred what Moses had related as the beginning of the creation of the world. For Moses wrote thus: "In the beginning God created the heaven and the earth," then the sun, and the moon, and the stars. For having learned this in Egypt, and having been much taken with what Moses had written in the Genesis of the world, he fabled that Vulcan had made in the shield of Achilles a kind of representation of the creation of the world. For he wrote thus:—

> "There he described the earth, the heaven, the sea,
> The sun that rests not, and the moon full-orb'd;
> There also, all the stars which round about,
> As with a radiant frontlet, bind the skies."

And he contrived also that the garden of Alcinous should preserve the likeness of Paradise, and through this likeness he represented it as ever-blooming and full of all fruits. For thus he wrote:—

> "Tall thriving trees confess'd the fruitful mould;
> The reddening apple ripens here to gold.
> Here the blue fig with luscious juice o'erflows,
> With deeper red the full pomegranate glows;
> The branch here bends beneath the weighty pear,
> And verdant olives flourish round the year.
> The balmy spirit of the western gale

Eternal breathes on fruits, untaught to fail;
Each dropping pear a following pear supplies,
On apples, figs on figs arise.
The same mild season gives the blooms to blow,
The buds to harden, and the fruits to grow.
Here order'd vines in equal ranks appear,
With all th' united labors of the year.
Some to unload the fertile branches run,
Some dry the blackening clusters in the sun,
Others to tread the liquid harvest join.
The groaning presses foam with floods of wine.
Here are the vines in early flower descry'd
Here grapes discolored on the sunny side,
And there in autumn's richest purple dy'd."

Do not these words present a manifest and clear imitation of what the first prophet Moses said about Paradise? And if anyone wish to know something of the building of the tower by which the men of that day fancied they would obtain access to heaven, he will find a sufficiently exact allegorical imitation of this in what the poet has ascribed to Otus and Ephialtes. For of them he wrote thus:—

"Proud of their strength, and more than mortal size,
The gods they challenge, and affect the skies.
Heav'd on Olympus tottering Ossa stood;
On Ossa, Pelion nods with all his wood."

And the same holds good regarding the enemy of mankind who was cast out of heaven, whom the Sacred Scriptures call the Devil, a name which he obtained from his first devilry against man; and if anyone would attentively consider the matter, he would find that the poet, though he certainly never mentions the name of "the devil," yet gives him a name from his wickedest action. For the poet, calling him Ate, says that he was hurled from heaven by their god, just as if he had a distinct remembrance of the expressions which Isaiah the prophet had uttered regarding him. He wrote thus in his own poem: —

> "And, seizing by her glossy locks
> The goddess Ate, in his wrath he swore
> That never to the starry skies again,
> And the Olympian heights, he would permit
> The universal mischief to return.
> Then, whirling her around, he cast her down
> To earth. She, mingling with all works of men,
> Caused many a pang to Jove."

Chapter XXIX.—Origin of Plato's doctrine of form.

And Plato, too, when he says that form is the third original principle next to God and matter, has manifestly received this suggestion from no other source than from Moses, having learned, indeed, from the words of Moses the name of form, but not having at the same time been instructed by the initiated, that without mystic insight it is impossible to have any distinct knowledge of the writings of Moses. For Moses wrote that God had spoken to him regarding the tabernacle in the following words: "And thou shalt make for me according to all that I show thee in the mount, the pattern of the tabernacle." And again:

"And thou shalt erect the tabernacle according to the pattern of all the instruments thereof, even so shalt thou make it." And again, a little afterwards: "Thus then thou shalt make it according to the pattern which was showed to thee in the mount." Plato, then, reading these passages, and not receiving what was written with the suitable insight, thought that form had some kind of separate existence before that which the senses perceive, and he often calls it the pattern of the things which are made, since the writing of Moses spoke thus of the tabernacle: "According to the form showed to thee in the mount, so shalt thou make it."

Chapter XXX.—Homer's knowledge of man's origin.

And he was obviously deceived in the same way regarding the earth and heaven and man; for he supposes that there are "ideas" of these. For as Moses wrote thus, "In the beginning God created the heaven and the earth," and then subjoins this sentence, "And the earth was invisible and unfashioned," he thought that it was the pre-existent earth which was spoken of in the words, "The earth was," because Moses said, "And the earth was invisible and unfashioned;" and he thought that the earth, concerning which he says, "God created the heaven and the earth," was that earth which we perceive by the senses, and which God made according to the pre-existent form. And so also, of the heaven which was created, he thought that the heaven which was created—and which he also called the firmament—was that creation which the senses perceive; and that the heaven which the intellect perceives is that other of which the prophet said, "The heaven of heavens is the Lord's, but the earth hath He given to the children of men." And so also concerning man: Moses first mentions the name of man, and then after many other creations he makes mention of the formation of man, saying, "And God made man, taking dust from the earth." He thought, accordingly, that the man first so named existed before the man who was made, and that he who was formed of the earth was afterwards made according to the pre-existent form. And that man was formed of earth, Homer, too, having discovered from the ancient and divine history which says, "Dust thou art, and unto dust shalt thou return," calls the lifeless body of Hector dumb clay. For in condemnation of Achilles dragging the corpse of Hector after death, he says somewhere:—

"On the dumb clay he cast indignity, Blinded with rage."

And again, somewhere else, he introduces Menelaus, thus addressing those who were not accepting Hector's challenge to single combat with becoming alacrity,—

"To earth and water may you all return,"—

resolving them in his violent rage into their original and pristine formation from earth. These things Homer and Plato, having learned in Egypt from the ancient histories, wrote in their own words.

Chapter XXXI.—Further proof of Plato's acquaintance with Scripture.

For from what other source, if not from his reading the writings of the prophets, could Plato have derived the information he gives us, that Jupiter drives a winged chariot in heaven? For he knew this from the following expressions of the prophet about the cherubim: "And the glory of the Lord went out from the house and rested on the cherubim; and the cherubim lift up their wings, and the wheels beside them; and the glory of the Lord God of Israel was over them above." And borrowing this idea, the magniloquent Plato shouts aloud with vast assurance, "The great Jove, indeed, driving his winged chariot in heaven." For from what other source, if not from Moses and the prophets, did he learn this and so write? And whence did he receive the suggestion of his saying that God exists in a fiery substance? Was it not from the third book of the history of the Kings, where it is written, "The Lord was not in the wind; and after the wind an earthquake, but the Lord was not in the earthquake; and after the earthquake a fire, but the Lord was not in the fire; and after the fire a still small voice?" But these things pious men must understand in a higher sense with profound and meditative insight. But Plato, not attending to the words with the suitable insight, said that God exists in a fiery substance.

Chapter XXXII.—Plato's doctrine of the heavenly gift.

And if anyone will attentively consider the gift that descends from God on the holy men, —which gift the sacred prophets call the Holy Ghost,—he shall find that this was announced under another name by Plato in the dialogue with Meno. For, fearing to name the gift of God "the Holy Ghost," lest he should seem, by following the teaching of the prophets, to be an enemy to the Greeks, he acknowledges, indeed, that it comes down from God, yet does not think fit to name it the Holy Ghost, but virtue. For so in the dialogue with Meno, concerning reminiscence, after he had put many questions regarding virtue, whether it could be taught or whether it could not be taught, but must be gained by practice, or whether it could be attained neither by practice nor by learning, but was a natural gift in men, or whether it comes in some other way, he makes this declaration in these very words: "But if now through this whole dialogue we have conducted our inquiry and discussion aright, virtue must be neither a natural gift, nor what one can receive by teaching, but comes to those to whom it does come by divine destiny." These things, I think, Plato having learned from the prophets regarding the Holy Ghost, he has manifestly transferred to what he calls virtue. For as the sacred prophets say that one and the same spirit is divided into seven spirits, so he also, naming it one and the same virtue, says this is divided into four virtues; wishing by all means to avoid mention of the Holy Spirit, but clearly declaring in a kind of allegory what the prophets said of the Holy Spirit. For to this effect he spoke in the dialogue with Meno towards the close: "From this reasoning, Meno, it appears that virtue comes to those to whom it does come by a divine destiny. But we shall know clearly about this, in what kind of way virtue comes to men, when, as a first step, we shall have set ourselves to investigate, as an independent inquiry, what virtue itself is." You see how he calls only by the name of virtue, the gift that descends from above; and yet he counts it worthy of inquiry, whether it is right that this [gift] be called virtue or some other thing, fearing to name it openly the Holy Spirit, lest he should seem to be following the teaching of the prophets.

Chapter XXXIII.—Plato's idea of the beginning of time drawn from Moses.

And from what source did Plato draw the information that time was created along with the heavens? For he wrote thus: "Time, accordingly, was created along with the heavens; in order that, coming into being together, they might also be together dissolved, if ever their dissolution should take place." Had he not learned this from the divine history of Moses? For he knew that the creation of time had received its original constitution from days and months and years. Since, then, the first day which was created along with the heavens constituted the beginning of all time (for thus Moses wrote, "In the beginning God created the heavens and the earth," and then immediately subjoins, "And one day was made," as if he would designate the whole of time by one part of it), Plato names the day "time," lest, if he mentioned the "day," he should seem to lay himself open to the accusation of the Athenians, that he was completely adopting the expressions of Moses. And from what source did he derive what he has written regarding the dissolution of the heavens? Had he not learned this, too, from the sacred prophets, and did he not think that this was their doctrine?

Chapter XXXIV.—Whence men attributed to God human form.

And if any person investigates the subject of images, and inquires on what ground those who first fashioned your gods conceived that they had the forms of men, he will find that this also was derived from the divine history. For seeing that Moses history, speaking in the person of God, says, "Let Us make man in our image and likeness," these persons, under the impression that this meant that men were like God in form, began thus to fashion their gods, supposing they would make a likeness from a likeness. But why, ye men of Greece, am I now induced to recount these things? That ye may know that it is not possible to learn the true religion from those who were unable, even on those subjects by which they won the admiration of the heathen, to write anything original, but merely propounded by some allegorical device in their own writings what they had learned from Moses and the other prophets.

Chapter XXXV.—Appeal to the Greeks.

The time, then, ye men of Greece, is now come, that ye, having been persuaded by the secular histories that Moses and the rest of the prophets were far more ancient than any of those who have been esteemed sages among you, abandon the ancient delusion of your forefathers, and read the divine histories of the prophets, and ascertain from them the true religion; for they do not present to you artful discourses, nor speak speciously and plausibly—for this is the property of those who wish to rob you of the truth—but use with simplicity the words and expressions which offer themselves, and declare to you whatever the Holy Ghost, who descended upon them, chose to teach through them to those who are desirous to learn the true religion. Having then laid aside all false shame, and the inveterate error of mankind, with all its bombastic parade and empty noise, though by means of it you fancy you are possessed of all advantages, do you give yourselves to the things that profit you. For neither will you commit any offence against your fathers, if you now show a desire to betake yourselves to that which is quite opposed to their error, since it is likely enough that they themselves are now lamenting in Hades, and repenting with a too late repentance; and if it were possible for them to show you thence what had befallen them after the termination of this life, ye would know from what fearful ills they desired to deliver you. But now, since it is not possible in this present life that ye either learn from them, or from those who here profess to teach that philosophy which is falsely so called, it follows as the one thing that remains for you to do, that, renouncing the error of your fathers, ye read the prophecies of the sacred writers, not requiring from them unexceptionable diction (for the matters of our religion lie in works, not in words), and learn from them what will give you life everlasting. For those who bootlessly disgrace the name of philosophy are convicted of knowing nothing at all, as they are themselves forced, though unwillingly, to confess, since not only do they disagree with each other, but also expressed their own opinions sometimes in one way, sometimes in another.

Chapter XXXVI.—True knowledge not held by the philosophers.

And if "the discovery of the truth" be given

among them as one definition of philosophy, how are they who are not in possession of the true knowledge worthy of the name of philosophy? For if Socrates, the wisest of your wise men, to whom even your oracle, as you yourselves say, bears witness, saying, "Of all men Socrates is the wisest"—if he confesses that he knows nothing, how did those who came after him profess to know even things heavenly? For Socrates said that he was on this account called wise, because, while other men pretended to know what they were ignorant of, he himself did not shrink from confessing that he knew nothing. For he said, "I seem to myself to be wisest by this little particular, that what I do not know, I do not suppose I know." Let no one fancy that Socrates ironically feigned ignorance, because he often used to do so in his dialogues. For the last expression of his apology which he uttered as he was being led away to the prison, proves that in seriousness and truth he was confessing his ignorance: "But now it is time to go away, I indeed to die, but you to live. And which of us goes to the better state, is hidden to all but God." Socrates, indeed, having uttered this last sentence in the Areopagus, departed to the prison, ascribing to God alone the knowledge of those things which are hidden from us; but those who came after him, though they are unable to comprehend even earthly things, profess to understand things heavenly as if they had seen them. Aristotle at least—as if he had seen things heavenly with greater accuracy than Plato—declared that God did not exist, as Plato said, in the fiery substance (for this was Plato's doctrine) but in the fifth element, air. And while he demanded that concerning these matters he should be believed on account of the excellence of his language, he yet departed this life because he was overwhelmed with the infamy and disgrace of being unable to discover even the nature of the Euripus in Chalcis. Let not any one, therefore, of sound judgment prefer the elegant diction of these men to his own salvation, but let him, according to that old story, stop his ears with wax, and flee the sweet hurt which these sirens would inflict upon him. For the above-mentioned men, presenting their elegant language as a kind of bait, have sought to seduce many from the right religion, in imitation of him who dared to teach the first men polytheism. Be not persuaded by these persons, I entreat you, but read the prophecies of the sacred writers. And if any slothfulness or old hereditary superstition prevents you from reading the prophecies of the holy men through which you can be instructed regarding the one only God, which is the first article of the true religion, yet believe him who, though at first he taught you polytheism, yet afterwards preferred to sing a useful and necessary recantation—I mean Orpheus, who said what I quoted a little before; and believe the others who wrote the same things concerning one God. For it was the work of Divine Providence on your behalf, that they, though unwillingly, bore testimony that what the prophets said regarding one God was true, in order that, the doctrine of a plurality of gods being rejected by all, occasion might be afforded you of knowing the truth.

Chapter XXXVII.—Of the Sibyl.

And you may in part easily learn the right religion from the ancient Sibyl, who by some kind of potent inspiration teaches you, through her oracular predictions, truths which seem to be much akin to the teaching of the prophets. She, they say, was of Babylonian extraction, being the daughter of Berosus, who wrote the Chaldæan History; and when she had crossed over (how, I know not) into the region of Campania, she there uttered her oracular sayings in a city called Cumæ, six miles from Baiæ, where the hot springs of Campania are found. And being in that city, we saw also a certain place, in which we were shown a very large basilica cut out of one stone; a vast affair, and worthy of all admiration. And they who had heard it from their fathers as part of their country's tradition, told us that it was here she used to publish her oracles. And in the middle of the basilica they showed us three receptacles cut out of one stone, in which, when filled with water, they said that she washed, and having put on her robe again, retires into the inmost chamber of the basilica, which is still a part of the one stone; and sitting in the middle of the chamber on a high rostrum and throne, thus proclaims her oracles. And both by many other writers has the Sibyl been mentioned as a prophetess, and also by Plato in his Phædrus. And Plato seems to me to have counted prophets divinely inspired when he read her prophecies. For he saw that what she had long ago predicted was accomplished; and on this account he expresses in the Dialogue with Meno his wonder at and admiration of prophets in the following terms: "Those whom we now call prophetic persons we should rightly name divine. And not least would we say that they are divine, and are raised to the prophetic ecstasy by the inspiration and possession of God, when they correctly speak of many and important matters, and yet know nothing of what they are saying," —plainly and manifestly referring to the prophecies of the Sibyl. For, unlike the poets who, after their poems are penned, have power to correct and polish, especially in the way of increasing the accuracy of their verse, she was filled indeed with prophecy at the time of the inspiration, but as soon as the inspiration ceased, there ceased also the remembrance of all she had said. And this indeed was the cause why some only, and not all, the meters of the verses of the Sibyl were preserved. For we ourselves, when in that city, ascertained from our cicerone, who showed us the places in which she used to prophesy, that there was a certain coffer made of brass in which they said that her remains were preserved. And besides all else which they told us as they had heard it from their fathers, they said also that they who then took down her prophecies, being illiterate persons, often went quite astray from the accuracy of the meters; and this, they said, was the cause of the want of meter in some of the verses, the prophetess having no remembrance of what she had said, after the possession and inspiration ceased, and the reporters having, through their lack of education, failed to record the meters with accuracy. And on this account, it is manifest that Plato had an eye to the prophecies of the Sibyl when he said this about prophets, for he said, "When they correctly speak of many and important matters, and yet know nothing of what they are saying.

Chapter XXXVIII.—Concluding appeal.

But since, ye men of Greece, the matters of the true religion lie not in the metrical numbers of poetry, nor yet in that culture which is highly esteemed among you, do ye henceforward pay less devotion to accuracy of meters and of language; and giving heed without contentiousness to the words of the Sibyl, recognize how great are the benefits which she will confer upon you by predicting, as she does in a clear and patent manner, the advent of our Savior Jesus Christ; who, being the Word of God, inseparable from Him in power, having assumed man, who had been made in the image and likeness of God, restored to us the knowledge of the religion of our ancient forefathers, which the men who lived after them abandoned through the bewitching counsel of the envious devil, and turned to the worship of those who were no gods. And if you still hesitate and are hindered from belief regarding the formation of man, believe those whom you have hitherto thought it right to give heed to, and know that your own oracle, when asked by someone to utter a hymn of praise to the Almighty God, in the middle of the hymn spoke thus, "Who formed the first of men, and called him Adam." And this hymn is preserved by many whom we know, for the conviction of those who are unwilling to believe the truth which all bear witness to. If therefore, ye men of Greece, ye do not esteem the false fancy concerning those that are no gods at a higher rate than your own salvation, believe, as I said, the most ancient and time-honored Sibyl, whose books are preserved in all the world, and who by some kind of potent inspiration both teaches us in her oracular utterances concerning those that are called gods, that have no existence; and also clearly and manifestly prophesies concerning the predicted advent of our Savior Jesus Christ, and concerning all those things which were to be done by Him. For the knowledge of these things will constitute your necessary preparatory training for the study of the prophecies of the sacred writers. And if any one supposes that he has learned the doctrine concerning God from the most ancient of those whom you name philosophers, let him listen to Ammon and Hermes: to Ammon, who in his discourse concerning God calls Him wholly hidden; and to Hermes, who says plainly and distinctly, "that it is difficult to comprehend God, and that it is impossible even for the man who can comprehend Him to declare Him to others." From every point of view, therefore, it must be seen that in no other way than only from the prophets who teach us by divine inspiration, is it at all possible to learn anything concerning God and the true religion.

www.ingramcontent.com/pod-product-compliance
Lightning Source LLC
Chambersburg PA
CBHW071254070526
44583CB00017B/2467